MY PRAYER FOR PEACE

by

Richard Doiron

MY PRAYER FOR PEACE
By Richard Doiron
First Edition 2002

ISBN 1-894372-18-12
Poetry – Canadian – Peace

Edited by Joan Allison

Cover Art by Andrew Holmes,
England. www.mowendi.com
mowi@mowendi.com

Cover Design
Dawn Drew – INK Graphic Design

Typesetting
Sonya Sullivan

Printed and bound in Canada

DREAMCATCHER PUBLISHING INC.
Suite 306 Dockside, 1 Market Square
Saint John New Brunswick Canada E2L 4Z6
www.dreamcatcher.nb.ca

Dedicated to the memory of:
Imelda (Arsenault) Doiron
1918-2001
Whose life was a living prayer

Acknowledgements

I acknowledge the following persons
who, one way or another, have been instrumental
in the production of this book:

Mike Wedge; Cheryl Newhook; Melanie Doiron;
Dan Doiron; Esla Bynoe Ewida; Cheryl Stachura;
Cindy van den Bosch; James Foster; Jesus Salgueiro; Bruce
Millican & Bonnie Kilborn; Ray & Viola Cormier;
The Hon. Marilyn Trenholme Counsell; The Hon.
Margaret Norrie McCain; The Right Honourable Adrienne
Clarkson;
Dr. Eldon Hay; Bill & Jeannine Wedge; Michael B. Sullivan;
Leo Noel; Dr. Theresia Quigley & Louis Quigley;
the Doiron Family; & Pauline Léger.

A special recognition to Canada's First Nations, from whom
I continue to learn so much about the Spirit.

A most sincere thank you to Dan Ennis, Grand Chief, the
Maliseet
First Nation; Robert Levy, Chief, the Mi'kmaq First Nation.

A most sincere thank you to Mr. Andrew Holmes,
West Yorkshire, England, artist extraordinaire.
In this case, I daresay, you can tell a book by its cover.

To DreamCatcher Publishing: Elizabeth Margaris; Yvonne
Wilson;
Joan Allison; and Dawn Drew, a most sincere thank you.

-Richard Doiron

Foreword

I have known Richard Doiron longer than I have known
poetry. In fact, it would be accurate to say that I do not
know poetry in a broad sense. However, I do know what I
like, and I like words that come from the heart, flow like
blood, and assault the senses. This is what the words of
Richard Doiron do. They can sting like the pain of a
broken heart; they can lift the spirits like newfound love—
sometimes all in the same verse.

As a sculptor takes a piece of clay and fashions it into a
thing of beauty, so does Richard create things of beauty
with his words. This is Richard's gift, a gift that has not
been squandered on this prolific writer—he uses it during
every waking moment; at times he even uses it in his sleep.
The best gifts are meant to be shared, and this is what
Richard does; he shares his gift for words and, in so
doing, he shares himself.

When you read the poems of Richard Doiron, you will
often see a reflection of yourself. I am sure Richard
intends it to be so. I am not sure, though, that he realizes
just how much his words reflect himself. The pages that
follow are more than reflection, however. They are nothing
less than a journey through the human heart.

James Foster,
Editor at large, the *Times & Transcript*
Moncton, New Brunswick, Canada
Telephone(506) 859-7133

TABLE OF CONTENTS

TOMORROW'S WORLD

This is tomorrow's world.
Come. Let us take up the task:
Standing tall among the Trees;
Reaching up to touch the Sky;
Bending low to taste the Earth;
Drinking deep from out the Source;
Breathing fast and free the Air of Life;
Stretching far to stir a Friend;
Fearing not the least of things -

The future -such promise! -:
The dreams of our Fathers, Grandfathers,
And all those who came before, before,
And before, now upon us and in our hands!

This is tomorrow's world.
Come. Let us take up the task:
Hand in hand into even greater
Tomorrows still; forever Children
Before Elders, forever Elders before
Children; forever humbled before
The Threshold and the Throne!

This is tomorrow's world.
Come. Let us explore the meaning.
Indeed, in the newness of this day,
Let us move beyond the realm of dreams,
A Body for a Body, gone as from Beings, lost,
Adrift on a great sea of conflict
And confusion, to Beings found,
Embarked, once and for all, upon
The safe and solid ground
Of Everlasting Peace!

CREDO

Speak in simple terms.
Seek to be understood.
Strive for clarity.
And be patient.
Keep an open mind, and
Show empathy. Be kind.
The world needs gentleness.
Touch it with loving hands.
Remember: where you go,
Others have surely gone,
As others will surely follow.
Cry, if you must, but seek,
After, the laughter.
When you balance things,
You will always find more good
Than bad, more laughter
Than tears, more joy
Than sorrow.
This is your world, and
The world is also what you
Make it. It is all quite
Simple, really –as simple
As the terms you use.
Go, then, and speak softly.

EAGLE SPIRIT
(a prayer)

Set me free, O Lord.
Give me wings
That I may fly.
Make me then soar,
To span the distances,
Near and far,
Held aloft by Your Loving-Kindness.
Make my wings beat
Over vast and troubled regions,
That an unbelieving world
Might be made a witness
To Your Powers.
It is my humble wish
To carry forth the Message
Of Your Love and Freedom.
Speed me on my way, O Lord.
It is my desire to soar,
To sing, and to serve.
Make me then fly, my utterances
Your Wondrous Melodies,
That I may promote Your Cause
As might a bird
Your lofty skies.

PRAYER FOR UNITY

O Giver Most Gracious!
O My God!
You Who occupy, by Your
Own Decree, the Throne
Of Thrones, by Whose Thought
The universe became reality,
Proffer upon us such unique
Vision as will induce
Us to declare:
"As this God is in all that is,
Who brought it all into being,
So are we, therefore a part
Of this God, united,
One to the other,
Without exception!"

PERSONAL PRAYER

Let me live in the moment, O my God.
Let me spread my wings and fly.
Let me transcend my fears.
Let me love.

By the dust of Your Earth was I given form.
By Your Breath was I given life.
By Your Wisdom was I given thought.
By Your Love was I given heart.

From Your Great Unknown the wonder of my soul;
From the wonder of my soul my reverence;
From my reverence mention of Your Name;
From mention of Your Name my destiny.

Deny me not Your Wise Counsels, O my God.
Deny me not the Power and the Glory.
Deny me not the stirring in my soul.
Deny me not the endlessness of time.

Let me live in the moment, O my God.
Let me spread my wings and fly.
Let me transcend my fears.
Let me love.

LOVE'S THE ANSWER

Despite the pledges so often made
The best of intentions as our base
What's to suggest we've made the grade
If love's not given its proper place

And what is proper and what is right
With the days that pass and years that fly
But that we'd answer, with great delight
That nothing precious has passed us by

And what's the measure of precious things
And what's the meter that sets apart
Is it the glimmer of diamond rings
That springs eternal the human heart

I say deeper, yes, far deeper still
The blazing banner that stems our hopes
Above and beyond mere human will
Abides the spirit that envelops

This, then, the promise – the tie that binds
To render lithe the dreadful dancer
No greater treasure the seeker finds
Than to apprise that love's the answer

PRAYER FOR JUSTICE

O my God! O my God!
You Who are the Embodiment
Of the Purest Light, grant that I
May be a reflection of the Orb
Of Your Utmost Reality!

O Most Judicious Judge!
Assess me not so much
For that which I am,
But incline me to that
Which affords me a semblance
Of You, that I, verily, may come to look
Upon my neighbour
As I myself would be looked upon,
Luminescent as You
Are Luminescent,
Merciful as You
Are Merciful,
Just as You
Are Just!

Richard Doiron

VIGILANCE

Let me be vigilant, O my Lord.
Let me beware that I not
Offend or obstruct.
Assist me in my vigilance.

O my Lord, grant that I should
Set my eyes only upon that
Which is meet, that my ears
Should hear only that which
Is seemly, that my lips
Should utter only that which
Is tender and true.

Where I might cast my gaze
Upon degradation, cause my eyes
To grow dim.
Where I might find my hearing
A jeopardy, cause silence
To occur.
Where I might speak ill
Of anyone, cause my speech
To fail.

Let me be vigilant, O my Lord.
Let me beware.

THE SPARROW
(a prayer)

I pray, behold my words, O my God!
I come to you, a sparrow, broken
Of heart and of spirit, my shattered
Self as lead upon the ground.
See me grieved and overwhelmed,
My wounded wings useless
To carry me aloft,
And I with such a longing
For the wonder of Your skies!
And what is a sparrow
But that it should fly!
And what is a prayer
But that it should reach
Its destiny!
O Most Bounteous Beauty!
Grant that I may rise,
That I may soar,
That I may overcome.
I pray, give life to these,
My wings, renew my heart,
Uplift my spirit,
Make me complete and whole!

MY MIND COULD BE A GARDEN

My mind could be a garden
Where a wealth of wonders grow
With bird and bee come dancing
Pollinating every row

My mind could be a canvas
Such blossoms bold and teeming
Myself to pinch and waken from
This awesome state of dreaming

My mind could be a meadow
Where the yearling comes to lie
Where welcome peace is ageless
Where the ancients came to die

My mind could be a garden
With a beauty yet unflawed
Each and every seed there planted
By the very hand of God

LET US WALK THROUGH THIS DAY

Let us walk through this day
Together and in abiding peace,
O my God.

Let us make of this day,
As unto all others,
A new beginning.

Let us look at the dawn
With the eyes of the newly-born,
Innocent, and unsullied.

Let us to look at the noonday sun
With the eyes of reason, in
Consultation and compromise.

Let us to look at the night
With the eyes of the Elder, calm,
Reflective, and unafraid.

Let us to walk through this day,
As through the fullness of life,
With a fair measure of leisure,
Laughter, and love.

Let us walk through this day
In remembrance of You, O my God.

Let us walk through this day
In remembrance.

Let us walk through this day.

I'VE SEEN THE SNOW

I've seen the snow, the valley, and the veil;
I've known the hue that's fashioned to be white;
I've felt the fluff upon the cottontail,
And tasted love, that's gloried in the light!

Myself as much then altered of the theme –
To seek as yet the folly of the fleece:
We go within and, there, we find the dream,
Which leads us then into Eternal Peace!

Upon the scene the setting of the stage,
The way thus cleared that I should play a part:
I spoke such words as written on the page;
But, best of all, I hearkened to my heart!

I've seen the milk, the oyster, and the dove –
The best of white: the colour that was Love!

WHERE ANGELS PLAYED

I came upon my God one blesséd night,
And down upon my knees, so quick to bend,
Myself in awe, but oh! to comprehend!
Upon such wonder gazed the neophyte,
Whereat the heaven's range, in pure delight,
The harps, whereon the angels played, no end,
Eternity their ally and their friend –
An Honour Guard before Almighty Might!

And, in that place, I spoke to God, and said,
In words I knew my God to understand :
"If counted now myself among the dead,
Would Thou be kind and therefore take my hand?"
But God, in silence, ushered me away,
For angels there had symphonies to play!

CELEBRATION

O Spirit Most Holy!
O my God!
You who bring together such
Souls as these, in love and
In unity, grant that these two
Hearts should beat as one,
That these voices should be heard
In harmony, that these two Spirits
Be bonded through the endlessness
Of time!
O Most Generous Giver!
Give unto these two the Gifts
Of Continued Love, the Gem
Of Intimacy, the Treasure
Of Contentment, the Blessing
Of Maturity!
O Presence Most Potent!
Give unto these two
The Candlelight of Constancy,
The Sacred Wine of Wonder,
The Music of Mystery!
Give unto these two Your Most
Excellent Counsels, that their lives
Might be a Celebration, Continuous,
Connected, and Clear.

MY GOD, MY GOD
(a prayer)

As now the sun takes up the sky,
As now the wind a rustling makes,
As now the bird is on the fly,
As now the spark in me that wakes,
    I call Your Name,
    My God, my God!

As now the child begins to stir,
As now the world is well renewed,
As now the mind becomes a blur,
As now the heart becomes unglued,
    I call Your Name,
    My God, my God!

As now this one takes up his place,
As now the Earth becomes the prize,
As now the Moon's upon my face,
As now the Star's before my eyes,
    I call Your Name,
    My God, my God!

As now the days give in to years,
As now the years to decades swell,
As now the life that disappears,
As now the me that's but a shell,
    I call Your Name,
    My God, my God!

As now the sound, the trumpet's blast,
As now the voice of angels heard,
As now I've crossed that ocean vast,
As now I've but one single word,
    I call Your Name,
    My God, my God!

A MOTHER'S PRAYER

All praise be to You, O Lord,
You Who have given life to the
Givers of life, through the most
Wondrous legacy of children.

I am a mother and therefore
A giver of life, if, unlike You,
Who are Self-Sufficient, I am,
Of myself, no more than a tree in winter,
Leafless, dormant, but that You should
Breathe the breath of life
Within me.

O my Lord!
You Who have willed it so
That life should come in answer
To itself, in these tiny forms,
Grant Your Most Excellent Favours,
That I, through this Mission Most
Magical and Magnificent,
Might be as a beacon, offering up
Guidance, whereby my own legacy
Should be self-evident, but, also, whereby
The calling of Your Name
Should be my gift most appropriate
And enduring!

SUPPLICATION

God bless and keep me.
Grant that Peace
Should permeate
My home.
Allow herein for the presence
Of stranger as well as of intimate.
Guide me. Protect me.
Inspire my every thought.
Make of me a servant,
In such wise
As to bring notice
Unto my peers.
Cause me that I should reflect,
Attuned to You
In my day as well as in
My night.
Avail me of Love.
Deny me of dissension.
Remove my fears.
Empower me to be myself,
That, in the fullness of my reality,
I may bring honour
Unto myself, unto my home,
Unto my neighbour,
Above all, unto Your Name!

IF THE SHEEP HAVE WOOL

If a fly has wings among other things
And the rivers can run dry
Then the clouds above can be filled with love
As the raindrops in the sky

If the stars can light all the world at night
And the moon in silver gleam
Then a tree can bend and address me friend
In the wonder of my dream

If the sheep have wool when the winter's full
And there's flags to be unfurled
Then there's cause for hope on the bigger scope
And for peace around the world

FAMILY PRAYER

God bless and keep this Family,
Which, by Your Own Decree,
Has come into being.
Make of us, Each and Everyone,
As pillars unto a fortress,
That we may, all, united, stand,
Sturdy and strong.
Give unto us a meet portion
Of the Ocean of Your Wealth,
That we may be sated
And satisfied.
Guard us from distance and discord,
That, with the passing of time,
We may better discover
And discern
The fullness of ourselves,
Both as individuals
And as that Renowned Reality
The Name of Which is Family!

REMEMBRANCE

Remember me always, O my Lord.
Remember me in my daytime
As in the night season, in my joy
As in my sorrow, in my pride
As in my humility.
Remember me when I, myself,
Am found forgetful,
Remembering me as only You
Can remember, teaching me, all
The while, that I, too,
Should become adept at remembering.
Most of all, O Lord, make it
So that I should come to
Apprehend wherefore
The Source of the Most Great
Remembrance.

DANCE

Make me dance, O my God,
Forever a student, in ardor, tireless,
My ear ever so inclined to
The Great Symphony of Love and of Life!

O You Who are the Mystery
And the Melody, the Composer and
The Conductor, the Strings and
The Winds, how shall I remain unmoved,
And unmoving, at the Music of the Spheres,
While even such as the stone does utter
So joyous a sound, that this, too,
Is most assuredly deemed
As approval and applause!

O Mover of Mountains!
O Stepper of Steppers!
Compel me, that I should dance,
That I should make of others, likewise,
Dancers, whereby to show is to tell,
And whereby the rhapsody and the rapture
Should be proofs of my promise
And my prompting, my mission
And my mandate, my sustenance
And my support!

O Dancer Most Delightful!
O Artiste Most Adept!
Take me from the mundane
To the Magic, from the waning
To the Wonder, from the shadow
To the Stage!

THE POTTER'S WHEEL

O my God! O my God!
I am but as a lump of clay
Upon the Potter's Wheel, to be
Molded, and shaped, and made
Compliant to my Master's Touch.
Make of me as You will, Your Hand
At the Wheel, the Vision Your own.

O my God! O my God!
I submit and I surrender,
Bending to Your Will. Mold me.
Shape me. Make me the vessel of
Your choosing, my very self,
In my many guises, upon
Your Wheel, formless, lifeless,
Incomplete, but for Your Will,
For Your Vision, for Your Touch.

O my Master!
Give me form. Give me life.
Make me complete and whole.

CHILD OF THE UNIVERSE

Child of the Universe
Your dream upon a star
A million miles for you
Is far away from far

You are so special, child
There are no imitations
In the expanses of your mind
There are no limitations

The galaxies are loose
Allowing for your feet
While suns explode from overload
Oh such worlds you've come to meet

Child of the Universe
Your dream upon a star
You twinkle and you sprinkle
The particles you are

The meteors that fall
Are scattered and abound
They shower on the hour
This Universe around

Richard Doiron

MY PRAYER FOR PEACE

Whereas the wounded self can never do the work
Of the self healed, I pray that God will
give us guidance
And never forsake us, yes, even though the world
around us
Should crumble and should quake;

I pray for a kinder day, that reason will prevail,
That we might recover and recoup from wounds too
severe
For mere mortals to contemplate and to bear;

I pray for peace in our homes and in our lands,
For the Mercy of all Creation to shower down upon
us,
That our worst of days and our best of days might be
difficult
To differentiate one from the other;

I pray for the Earth, the Mother of us all,
No more to be neglected, assaulted, and assailed;

I pray for the Sky, that the starry night
Once again might be seen to startle and to stir;

I pray for the Spring, the River, and the Sea,
The bodies of which are the Waters of Life;

I pray for the Four Directions, that the Races
Might come together, sharing a common vision
Of Compassion, Unity, Hope, and Love;

My Prayer for Peace

I pray for the Wind, that it should take our angry
words
And cause them to dissipate and to disappear;

I pray for the Oppressed, that their woes
Might be a thing of the past;

I pray for Equality, that the Sexes might know
Of a Justice unfettered and without fail;

I pray for the Weak, that they might be
strengthened,
And for the Strong, that they might be tempered;

I pray for the Ailing and for the Angels of Mercy
Attending to their ills;

I pray for the Tearful and for the drying of tears,
That Hearts might be healed and Closures might be
found;

I pray for the Life of Each and Everyone, that the
Life
Of Each and Everyone might be promoted,
perceived,
And portrayed, as an Endless Prayer.

Richard Doiron

BY MY SOUL (I NOW BELIEVE)

As the wind blew strong I could hear a song
As it whistled through the trees
Where the angels trod 'twas the voice of God
And it brought me to my knees

And the music rang as a chorus sang
And the voice grew louder still
And I knew right then in this world of men
That I'd never have my fill

Then the wind died down and the cap and gown
Were upon my very frame
While the sun burned hot like a lobster pot
And the rivers called my name

And the turtledove was a blaze of love
As it streaked across the sky
And the Earth was green like I'd never seen
And the stones began to cry

Then the silence grew that was overdue
And the dead began to rise
And I stood in awe at these things I saw
Now unveiled before my eyes

Then the wind arose like a door to close
When the guest is taking leave
And that parting breeze rearranged the trees
By my soul I now believe

I AM THE VOICE

I am the voice where voices seldom heard;
Let them to pale and walk away in fear:
I give to each and every single word
A certain twist the lot of them to hear!

I am the heart where heartless fellows mass;
Let them beware upon their ruthless perch:
My voice rings out so strong it shatters glass;
The priest himself now trembles in his church!

I am the soul where spirits sorely lack;
Let them abhor the very thought of me:
Though wolves decry the leader of the pack,
He comes to them, in time, their liberty!

I am the voice that rings out in the night;
Go tell the wounded ones they've heard it right!

Richard Doiron

MY WORLD OF PAINTS

My world of paints I splatter, like a child,
Across the blue, in patterns big and bold:
The colours run, they're seen as running wild,
And here we're lost when things are uncontrolled!

Great globs of green now fall upon the trees;
Upon the seas, the colours now run blue;
There's yellows flung, that bring me my knees,
The likes mere gold could never ever do!

There's blacks and whites and colours in-between,
Like browns and reds and mixtures not so clear,
Arrayed in rows the likes they've never seen,
And yet each one the child in me holds dear!

My world of paints I fling across the sky;
Ask children, all, they'll know the reasons why!

IT'S TIME FOR PEACE

It's time for peace in families everywhere;
It's in the home the story has its start:
Let us erect such castles in the air,
That we'll have touched the Essence of the Heart.

It's time for peace in cities far and wide –
On every block the building of the bond:
Let us propel our prejudice aside –
A model made into the Great Beyond.

It's time for peace across this mighty land;
Let parties, all, inside the Circle, talk:
Let each one take a neighbour by the hand,
The load made light upon that daily walk.

It's time for peace across this warring world,
The Light of Love now seen to be unfurled.

Richard Doiron

THE HEAVY HAND

Heavy is the hand of hate in the land
But to see the bombs explode
On this selfsame street where we set our feet
And a ways just down the road

It's a faulty mind that goes forward blind
And that causes so much woe
But the truth be known it's a heavy stone
When it's someone that we know

In this day and age it's on every page
And the press is running late
As we check the print there's that awful hint
That the world is filled with hate

And there's not one soul in the picture whole
To escape that hateful crime
Let the new day come we are rendered numb
When we read it one more time

And the problem is that the fault is his
That we deem the other side
Let the score be kept we have overslept
For the numbers that have died

When we finally rise and there's none denies
We'll inherit what's above
For that heavy hand's but a grain of sand
On the Ocean that is Love

XXX

THE TALKING CIRCLE

Come, friends, let us gather.
Let us assemble, and speak.
We have here the Talking Circle.
Great are its mysteries.
Come, then, let us be seated.
Let us see what comes of it.
Do you hear the silence?
The silence is the secret.
The secret is sacred.
Because of the Circle we have words.
With our words, we break the silence.
Breaking the silence releases
The secrets.
This is how the mysteries
Are revealed.
Mysteries are forever.
Come, then, let us gather.
Let us assemble, and speak.

Richard Doiron

FREEDOM SONG

People who are imprisoned by their thoughts
Have a need to imprison others by their actions.
Beware the cage, even with its doors open,
For what is a cage but an entrapment.

Your freedom is more than flight; it is the sky
Itself, as endless as forever.

If you must alight, be it not before the cage,
But atop of it, that the weight of your understanding
May cause it to shatter and to break.

Should you shatter the cage, see to it that its
bars and wires
Are dismantled, discarded, nevermore to hinder.

People who are imprisoned by their thoughts
Have a need to imprison others by their actions.

Avoid these, that you may avoid imprisonment,
Yes, even the prospect of imprisonment.

Meanwhile, in your freedom, strive to set
others free, that they
May fly as the birds fly and sing as the angels sing.

Remember: heaven is upon this Earth, but that we
Have forgotten how to fly.

Fly, then. Fly. And sing, too, sing to the
top of your voice.
Be even as the birds and the angels are.
It is yours to do so.
So it must be, for so it is written; so it is written
In the fullness of the sky.

PRAYER FOR AN ARTIST

Let me look upon the Winter's White, O my God,
And see, thereon, no less than the selfsame Colours
As I might perceive when the Rainbow comes,
Attired, as it is, in its Summer Wear!

Let me look upon the Darkened Night, O my God,
And see, therein, Your Majesty and Your Might,
As if, on this occasion, I had chanced upon
The Wonder and Warmth of the Noonday Sun!

Let me look upon my Endeavour, O my God,
And see, therein, no less, the Inspiration and the Art,
As would have moved the Mallet and the Maul,
Upon that day when David came to Life!

Let me look upon my Fellow Beings, O my God,
And see, therein, Your Purpose and Your Plan,
As to then suggest of my Insightful Eyes
The Mirror of the Most Eternal Soul!

IN A BETTER WORLD

In a better world there are flags unfurled
And a peace that reigns supreme
It's in efforts made that they've make the grade
And they've realized the dream

If we set to work and there's none that shirk
Sure that goal will be achieved
There's a peaceful side and it's not denied
But that, first, someone believed

Let us work as one till that job is done
And uphold the creeds that are
In the worlds of God there is nothing odd
If we wish upon a star

THE UNIVERSAL MIND

It speaks to me upon the break of day –
My thoughts advanced like hands upon the clock:
I apprehend some words along the way,
Which then resound, to hear me when I talk.

It speaks to me upon the nudge of noon –
The darling dove to cooing and to call:
My feet are firm, this moment opportune,
As I behold the Maker of it all.

It speaks to me upon the setting sun –
The wisest words from infants that implore:
The measured mile addresses everyone,
With God, no less, heard knocking at my door.

It speaks to me upon the lilt of Love,
Whereas I dream with angels up above.

Richard Doiron

WHEN THE WORD IS LOVE

When the word is love then it wears a glove
On a hand that reaches out
For the one that knows that's the way it goes
For that's what it's all about

As we're here to learn give us each a turn
Till that glove is worn right through
When the word is love then it wears a glove
That's forever made anew

THE MEETING PRAYER

O God, our God,
Creator of Earth and Sky,
Overseer of the Universe,
We implore of You, in Your
Grandeur and Your Majesty,
To grant us wisdom
And to keep us on track
As we venture forth
In this Gathering.
May it be with a portion
Of Your Eyes with Which
We see, a portion of Your Ears
With Which we hear, a portion
Of Your Tongue with Which
We speak.
May this Meeting
Reflect understanding,
And may this understanding
Be a tribute.
May the absolute basis
For this Assembly
Be Love.
May there be unity
Of Mind and of Spirit.
And may the goal be common:
To be found worthy
Of so precious a Moment,
Forever
In Your Presence,
In Peace,
Rejoicing.

Richard Doiron

THE SEEKER'S PRAYER

I come to You as a seeker, O my God.
Assist me, then, that I should well discern
The true from the false, the chaff from the grain,
The beauty from the beast.

I come to You as a child, O my God, innocent,
And unsullied; be then to me as a mother's bosom,
That I should drink from the Milk of Your Infinite
Wisdom, that I should neither hunger, nor thirst, but,
Rather, that I should be wrapped in Your Warmth
And Your Wonder, sated and satisfied, in no wise,
Therefore, seeking elsewhere, supposing
A surrogate ever to suffice.

I come to You as an adult, O my God, placing
Before You my burden and my bane, my duty
And my dream, my secret and my sorrow,
Pleading my case, that You might hearken and hear,
Consider and clarify, decide and direct.

I come to You as a friend, O my God, seeking
That I might find, knocking that the door might
Be opened, asking that I might receive, accepting
That no God is there but You, the Help in Peril,
The Self-Subsisting.

I come to You as a seeker of truth, O my God,
Prompted by Your Promise and Your Pledge, Your
Message and Your meaning, Your Nearness
And Your Name.

HUMILITY PRAYER

**I come to You in reverence and in awe,
O my God, to have touched upon Your
Mystery and Your Might**

in

**the people I have known,
the places I have been,
the things I have seen.**

**I come to You in gratitude and in joy,
O my God, to have been blessed by Your
Light and Your Love**

in

**the Reality of Your Revelations,
the Majesty of Your Monarchs,
the Heralds and Hosts from on High.**

**I come to You in confidence and in trust,
O my God, to have been promised Your
Kingdom and Your Keeping**

in

**the Words of the Most Wise,
the Hardships of the Most Holy,
the Dawning of Their New Day.**

Richard Doiron

THE CHILDREN OF THE LIGHT

Behold this day the Children of the Light!
The eyes that see the haloes well discern:
Upon the Mount, in colours lily-white,
Such meetings held that Time dared not adjourn!

From ages past, the echoes of the Seers –
The "Keepers" come, to turn the thing around:
The neophytes are now the pioneers,
Their faithful feet upon this hallowed ground!

Take in the pies that they would make of mud,
And hear the words their "babbling" would bestow:
There's wisdom, now, that comes at us a flood,
And it's from babes, as pure as driven snow!

Behold this day the Children of the Star,
The Hands of Fate inside the cookie jar!

AS THE STARS DO GLEAM

As the stars do gleam we've designed the dream
Which we fit into our sphere
If the facts were known it's a writ in stone
And the reason that we're here

Where the soul is found it is hallowed ground
And it matters not the plane
All we've done in time is amend the rhyme
Now recited once again

It's a truth in full not a leg we pull
When we say there's nothing new
Let that line be crossed there is nothing lost
We but change, that's all we do

THE WALLS COME DOWN

The walls come down and we are made to see;
Beneath the stone forever is the print:
The road is long that paints Eternity,
But then the brush is always there, a hint.

The walls come down and shadows fall apart –
Far less the night a terror and a trial:
Tomorrow comes, a chapter we can chart,
An eager lot to go that extra mile.

The walls come down and peace is quickly made;
It's good to see the doing of the deed:
The student comes, in time, to make the grade,
But home, at first, is where we plant the seed.

The walls come down and things are rendered clear -
So sweet a smell that stirs the atmosphere.

I DIED FOR LOVE

I died for love in ages that are past
Come back to life to die a death anew
By Gracious God that I was made to last
And catapult this trampoline to you

Upon the scene, descended like a dart
That you should note the stature and the style
I've come to you a hammer in my heart
Once more, you see, to hold you for awhile

Behold the beam come bending to your brow
A tender kiss denoting of the dawn
Let aeons pass, you'll know me, as I'm now
For, in the end, I never will be gone

I died for love upon the former day
As I recall you saw me on my way

THERE IS A CIRCLE

There is a circle, O my God, an ever-expanding
circle, a circle drawing us all in,
Uniting us, insisting on our unity, refuting our
separateness, making valid Your
Great Purpose, invalidating our vain imaginings.

There is a circle, O my God, a circle the mandate of
which is Love, potent and pure,
With never a doubt and never a disputation, forever
decreed, insisted upon,
Established as "law," rendered concise and clear,
applicable to all, in both this world and in the world
to come.

There is a circle, O my God, a mighty circle,
apportioned to us with the conception of
Life, ours to uphold and entertain the duration of our
days, real yesterday, real
Today, irrefutable tomorrow.

There is a circle, O my God, a wondrous circle, a
circle which encompasses all, both
The seen and the unseen, a circle finding us here, this
day, bathed in beauty and
Bounty, the likes of which transcends our
understanding.

My Prayer for Peace

There is a circle, O my God, a celestial circle,
invoking in us a vision of victory,
Whereas, in our limitations, we might occasion a
doubt, accommodate a fear,
Presume ourselves in isolation.

There is a circle, O my God, a circle of security and
salvation, a circle of plenty, that
None should be in want, but that all should find
inclusion, secured with such bonds
That nothing, save Your Decree, could ever deter or
destroy.

There is a circle, O my God, a circle of light, in this
day made manifest, accepted as
Real, the same, named in Your Honour, which,
henceforth, shall lighten our load,
Afford us freedom, endear us, one and all, one to the
other, and which, most
Especially, shall aid and assist us in our collective and
conscious remembrance of You.

There is a circle, O my God, a Most Magical and
Majestic Circle, a circle no less real
Than the Thought Which wrought It, the same for us
never to disregard or
Disrespect, but, rather, wherein our refuge, our
rebirth, our redemption.

There is a circle, O my God, from Everlasting to
Everlasting.

ONE BLADE OF GRASS

One blade of grass, a solitary one,
Is proof of life, in any given sphere:
We have, on Earth, beneath the blazing sun,
Sufficient proof to say that life is here.

And what is life, forever, then, remains,
If yet to change a million million times:
The lowest form the highest rank attains,
Alike the vine, to see the way it climbs.

I say to you, behold the blade of grass,
Which, by itself, is taking up the green:
A million million years will come to pass,
To stretch no more than what you now have seen.

One blade of grass is all there needs to be,
As proof of life, therefore Eternity.

WHO PLY FOR PEACE

Who ply for peace are hard to criticize;
We need them more than any other kind:
No efforts made are we to minimize –
The least of it to take us from the bind.

We need to note the godsend that these are;
So rare a breed have set themselves apart:
Let them to strike upon the distant star,
It is such dream that opens up the heart.

With gentle hands, as tend the rarest rose,
We'll come to touch upon that Stately Stem:
Our days revised, we'll never come to blows,
But God knows well we'll need to be like them.

Who ply for peace have wisdom on their side,
A trait that hate can never override.

OF PAUPERS AND KINGS

No child was born but that it knows to dream,
With each, in turn, to conquer of the code,
Let all to see the gold and how it gleams,
And all to stand before the mother lode.

When, on the wings of time, the bird does fly,
To take its place and soar to endless height,
We must behold the wonder of the sky,
And make of it a passage and a rite.

From off the roof the rain yet falls anew,
To strike the ground a lesser kind of blow:
Let men be gods, among the lot of you,
Where, in the end, does all that water go?

No child is born but that it should have wings,
And this applies to paupers as to kings!

SIGNS AND WONDERS

This world abounds with wonders and with signs;
We have in us the docket to discern:
In all things known the fabric intertwines,
With all things gone forever to return.

No end is there to anything in sight –
Beyond this march the measure of the mile:
A shadow side to everything that's light,
A fool's a fool if only for awhile.

The Prophets come with Sacred Seal and Saw,
And we obtain the Windfall of the Word:
Let all to stand in challenge to the Law,
That day will come when all of us have heard.

We but behold the portion that we can,
Beyond the which the fullness of the Plan.

GOOD MORNING, CHILD

Good morning, Child, and how are you this day?
I'd like to hear the story of your dream:
I see in you someone who'll lead the way,
When drought sets in to cancel out the stream.

Good morning, Child, and how are you? I ask.
It's good to hear the story from the source:
I see in you someone who'll do the task,
When life itself is seeming out of course.

Good morning, Child, and how are you? I muse.
It's good to see the story that unfurls:
I see in you someone who'll fill the shoes,
When breaks the string that's holding up the pearls.

Good morning, Child, and how are you this morn?
Do tell me, please, the reasons you were born!

LET LOVE TO LIGHT

Let love to light upon the coldest heart,
That all may see the melting of the ice:
The robin sings and comes to play its part,
And never God is heard to tell it twice.

Let love to light upon the shaded wall,
That all may see the blazing of the sun:
The beaver dam yet sees the water fall,
For dams, as such, do not deter the run.

Let love to light upon the mighty foe,
That all may see the making of a friend:
There lingers yet the rain, out comes the bow,
Its arc so wide that it should seem no end.

Let love to light upon the distant star,
There shall be dreams for all to go that far.

BLESSÉD WOMAN

Blesséd are you O Woman of the World!
The heavens smile upon you every day :
You are the flag I see to be unfurled,
The voice of peace that's heard in every way!

Blesséd are you O Woman of the Light!
The angels sing, insisting that you shine :
Your crocheted cape was crocheted overnight,
The gods themselves the strands to intertwine!

Blesséd are you O Woman of the Arc!
You are the loop as surely as the sun :
Your ship's come in, it's time to disembark,
Your place to take, to dazzle everyone!

Blesséd are you O Woman of the Star!
Blesséd are you for being who you are!

THE BOOK OF LOVE

The book of love has pages we must fill;
It beckons us to splatter seas of ink:
The leaf is green that shows the chlorophyll,
The while the tome's reflecting how we think.

For sure we're known by entries that we make,
And each of us is surely to be known:
Take in the frost upon the wedding cake,
And think of seeds now waiting to be sown.

Recorded, then, upon this sheet of white,
Our very selves, the way we really are:
The deeds we do forever then the light,
By which we're known so very, very far.

The book of love? We're writing every page,
Which then but shows the ways we've come of age.

Richard Doiron

SELF-VALIDATION

I shower me with validating praise;
My inner child is happy as a lamb:
Contentment comes a constant to my days,
And fashions me the me I really am.

Oh how I love to gambol in the snow –
To sliding down the steepest hill of all –,
To be at ease where all the children go,
With life itself upon my beck and call.

What's past is passed and is to come no more,
For I'll but speak of it in words unkind:
Today, I live like never life before,
And I do clear the clutter from my mind.

A person grows, if given half a chance;
Now step aside, for I need room to dance.

THE CRYSTAL CROSS

I had this dream that left me at a loss –
To see the Lord, as if it were of old –,
Except to note that crystal was the cross,
While mocking words were scripted out of gold.

I saw Him writhe upon that fearsome frame –
Upward the eyes embracing of the Beam –,
But God was there, I heard that Holy Name,
And well I knew the meaning of my dream –:

Before my eyes, imbedded in the glass,
A row of spikes, that threatened to impale,
But this, I knew, would never come to pass,
For this was flawed, and it was meant to fail.

Each spike was sealed, if plainly to be spied –
Defined, at last, the folly and the fraud:
The thorns, as such, would never reach His side,
For, in the end, He'd walked away with God.

The Crystal Cross is high upon the Hill,
And, there, it stands, for everyone to see:
Tomorrow tells, the way it always will,
For such are Light, and Love, and Liberty.

Richard Doiron

THE BATTLEFIELD

The battlefield is not the place to weep –
In victory found the damper of defeat:
The eagle comes a slayer in our sleep,
Our wounded souls reminders when we meet.

Before the blows the nursing that we need –
That all be found too sated to be sore:
It's inner lack that's girding us with greed,
And so, my friends, the reasons that there's war.

Let us address the issues as they are –
Upon the hill the Herald of the Heart:
Let peace to press – a stranger to the scar –,
And we'll avoid the dagger and the dart.

The battlefield reveals to us but theft:
It shows no right; it only shows who's left.

LET'S PRAY FOR PEACE

Let's pray for peace till peace has come to pass;
We have in us the turning of the key:
The Spirit lives inside the looking glass;
We need but look and therefore will we see.

The universe is wondrous and it's wide,
And we were made to savor of the span:
The Book insists that all is sanctified,
The course made clear for all the caravan.

The trek we're on need not to decimate;
We have in us the drafting of the dove:
With open arms, let us to celebrate,
Proclaiming, then, the Light that's known as Love.

Let's pray for peace that peace should reign
Supreme,
Till children, all, have tasted of the Dream.

Richard Doiron

PEACE IN THE WORLD

The time has come to realize
The madness that is war
The time has come to put aside
Our guns forevermore
The awful things we've done
To wear that bloody crown
Have never picked us up
But only kept us down

(Chorus)
There must be peace in the world –
A brother for a brother
There must be peace in the world
Like there's never been another

We are a world emerging
We have the tools at hand
To build the greatest bridge
That love has ever spanned
We have no more excuses
For learning war at all
The peoples are united
Just hear their common call

(Chorus)
There must be peace in the world–
A brother for a brother
There must be peace in the world
Like there's never been another

GO BACK, MY CHILD

Go back, my child, to yesterday
You've many games as yet to play
Fear not the world and all its spite
Go back, my child, you have the right

Enchantment comes at any age
And who's to say and who's to gauge
Which games are meet and which are not
Go back, my child, and try the lot

Tomorrow comes at blinding speed
Some games you'll miss you badly need
Just bend an ear, you'll hear them call
Go back, my child, and play them all

-Richard Doiron

Richard Doiron

ON MY WORST OF DAYS

On my worst of days there's a child yet plays
And a sun that comes to shine
Let me fall apart with a broken heart
There's a hope that yet is mine

There's the puppy dog and the pollywog
And the butterfly in flight
There's the summer rain on my windowpane
And the stars that shine at night

There's the wind that blows and the scented rose
And the books I love to read
There's the healing heard in the loving word
Of a friend who knows my need

There's the rainbow's arc with its gentle spark
And the fishes in the stream
There's the baby's cry and the mother's sigh
As the two expand the dream

There's the grass that's green and the silver sheen
In the sky that brings the dawn
There's the robin's nest with the chick that's blessed
With its urge to carry on

There's the cricket's ring and the angel's wing
And the cooing of the dove
There's the hope I feel though my pains are real
In this life I've come to love

On my worst of days there's a child yet plays
And a sun that comes to shine
For the things I learn I must surely yearn
For there's hope; this hope is mine

About the Author:

Richard Doiron had his first poem published in 1970. "My Prayer for Peace"is his fourth book of poetry. His work has been read at the United Nations; at the World Congress of Poetry & Cultures; and he has taken first place in a world competition. He deems his greatest achievement that of being included in the world book, "Prayers for a Thousand Years," by invitation, alongside such luminaries as the Dalai Lama, Nelson Mandela and Desmond Tutu. While not easily categorized, he sees his work as spiritually based.

The native of Moncton, New Brunswick, Canada, had his first work published in 1964, in a letter to the Editor. Since that date, he has had an estimated 1000 such letters published across Canada. Since his daughter Melanie's birth, in 1982, he has addressed a daily journal to her, in what now amounts to a thirty thousand page diary. He easily writes an average of one thousand new poems yearly. The work "merely comes" to him, as he notes, and therefore he finds it hard to take credit for it. While publicly compared to a number of legendary poets, such as Emily Dickinson, the poet simply muses, wondering why comparisons are being made in the first place.

A French author also, both as a poet and an essayist, the author believes that literature bridges gaps. He considers it a privilege to share his work and does so regularly, these days employing the Internet, thereby reaching people around the globe. The feedback speaks for itself. Testimonials come from many lands, and, in many cases, from the highest offices in the land. A modest man, he simply says he knows who he is. And now, more and more, the world knows that as well.

Asked what inspires him, Richard Doiron sums it up in one word: Life.